Copyright © Suzanne Waldron, 2020

All rights reserved. No part of this publication may be reproduced, distributed, or transmitted in any form or by any means, including photocopying, recording, or other electronic or mechanical methods, without the prior written permission of the publisher, except in the case of brief quotations embodied in critical reviews and certain other noncommercial uses permitted by copyright law. For permission requests, write to the publisher, addressed "Attention: Permissions Coordinator," at the address below.

Suzanne Waldron
PO BOX 8007
Perth BC 6849
AUSTRALIA
www.suzannewaldron.com

Ordering Information:
Quantity sales. Special discounts are available on quantity purchases by corporations, associations, and others. For details, contact the publisher at the address above.

Printed in Australia by IngramSpark

Designed and Edited by Nathan Maddigan   www.nathanmaddigan.com

Cover art and internal illustrations by Natalia Fidyka   www.nataliafidyka.com

Author and Artist photography by Rachel Callander   www.rachelcallander.com

A catalogue record for this work is available from the National Library of Australia.

National Library of Australia Cataloguing-in-Publication data:
Creator:	Waldron, Suzanne.
Title:	Sleeping Giants: An invitation for deep thought. A philosophy for liberation. A calling to life / Suzanne Waldron.
ISBN:	978-0-6488833-0-2 (paperback)
Subjects:	Poetry.
	Self-Help & Personal Development.
	Mind, Body, Spirit.

First Edition

Disclaimer:
The material in this publication is of the nature of general comment only, and does not represent professional advice. It is not intended to provide specific guidance for particular circumstances and it should not be relied on as the basis for any decision to take action or not take action on any matter which it covers. Readers should obtain professional advice where appropriate, before making any such decisions. To the maximum extent permitted by law, the author and publisher disclaim all responsibility and liability to any person, arising directly or indirectly from any person taking or not taking action based on the information in this publication.

for me

for you

for us

an invitation

We each have a sleeping giant within us. Even those of us who consider ourselves fully awake. None of us are immune to life's darker sides: the distractions, the exhaustion, the dormancy of our greatness. We all hold within us the quiet places where dreams reside, deep needs emerge, and the greatest parts of us are formed.

The intention for this collection of thoughts and observations is that of an invitation, an offer to consider a deeper calling to life. So often I have found myself asking the question, "what is the point of it all?" In whirling storms of confusion, sometimes exciting, other times excruciating, there is always the question.

"What is the point?"

I imagine you've asked that question too.

Within us is a well. It is always there, always present. It holds for us insight and wisdom, gleaned from observations, stories, experiences – the magnitude of our lives.

Big or small. The giant inside us may be ready to wake up. To be validated and heard. To serve and to be of use. No matter the spectrum or size of the giant, it exists, and so then the opportunity stands before us.

This invitation doesn't assume anything about you, valued reader. It doesn't seek to label or preach. It doesn't forgo your history or experiences. It simply lays bare, reflections which come from near and far. Ancient writings, philosophy, faith, research, science, and art. Imagining this is a perfect time to be called upon, the intention is gentle. But, please know that this invitation does invite your response. It speaks to you and your giant.

Take what you need. Disregard the rest. Or perhaps, put the rest aside for a future time when that internal well needs a reinvigorating top up.

My dream is that this book lends itself to those times of searching. When the longing of deep meaning is calling to you. Perhaps something here in these pages may provide comfort, and resonance. And if your soul feels provoked towards momentum, may you take the steps that embellish life, and all that you hope for it to be.

Your giant awaits you. The world awaits your giant.

liberation

I'm wildly enthusiastic about philosophers, and when A.C. Grayling's description of a good life came across my field of vision, it made deep sense. In his book *Thinking of Answers*, he writes:

"It would be peace for all and freedom for each where 'freedom' means personal autonomy and mental liberation from prejudice, superstition, ignorance and fear.

Cynics will no doubt think this is a saccharine sentiment merely, If only on the grounds that it is unattainable and that one had better stick to the realities of a world in which the majority of people are trapped in economic and intellectual prisons made by history (and it's bequeathment of superstition, ignorance and fear), perpetuated and promoted by demagogues and the greedy and powerful.

The cynics are of course right about the realities, but that does not mean one should shrug ones shoulders and capitulate. There is something one can do to fight back, by taking part in the battle that underlies it all: the battle between those who see the truth and those who claim to have it..."

"...to summarise: the battle for peace and freedom is a battle about mindsets."

This passage has me wondering. As indeed life itself does. About compassion, freedom, liberation and hope.

That wondering is what this book is about.

love beauty creativity imagination fortitude resourcefulness joy virtuousness	*originating*
worth betrayal attachment grief regret blame uncertainty doubt jealousy	*forgetting*
tenderness gratitude curiosity forgiveness truth hope wisdom aloneness vulnerability quickening	*waking*
empathy kindness playfulness generosity discernment responsibility fairness serving calling	*liberating*

a splendid torch

"This is the true joy in life, the being used for a purpose
recognised by yourself as a mighty one;
the being a force of nature instead of a feverish,
selfish little clod of ailments and grievances
complaining that the world will not devote itself
to making you happy.

I am of the opinion that my life belongs to the whole
community, and as long as I live
it is my privilege to do for it whatever I can.

I want to be thoroughly used up when I die,
for the harder I work the more I live.
I rejoice in life for its own sake.

Life is no "brief candle" for me.
It is a sort of splendid torch which I have got hold of
for the moment, and I want to make it burn
as brightly as possible before handing it on
to future generations."

George Bernard Shaw

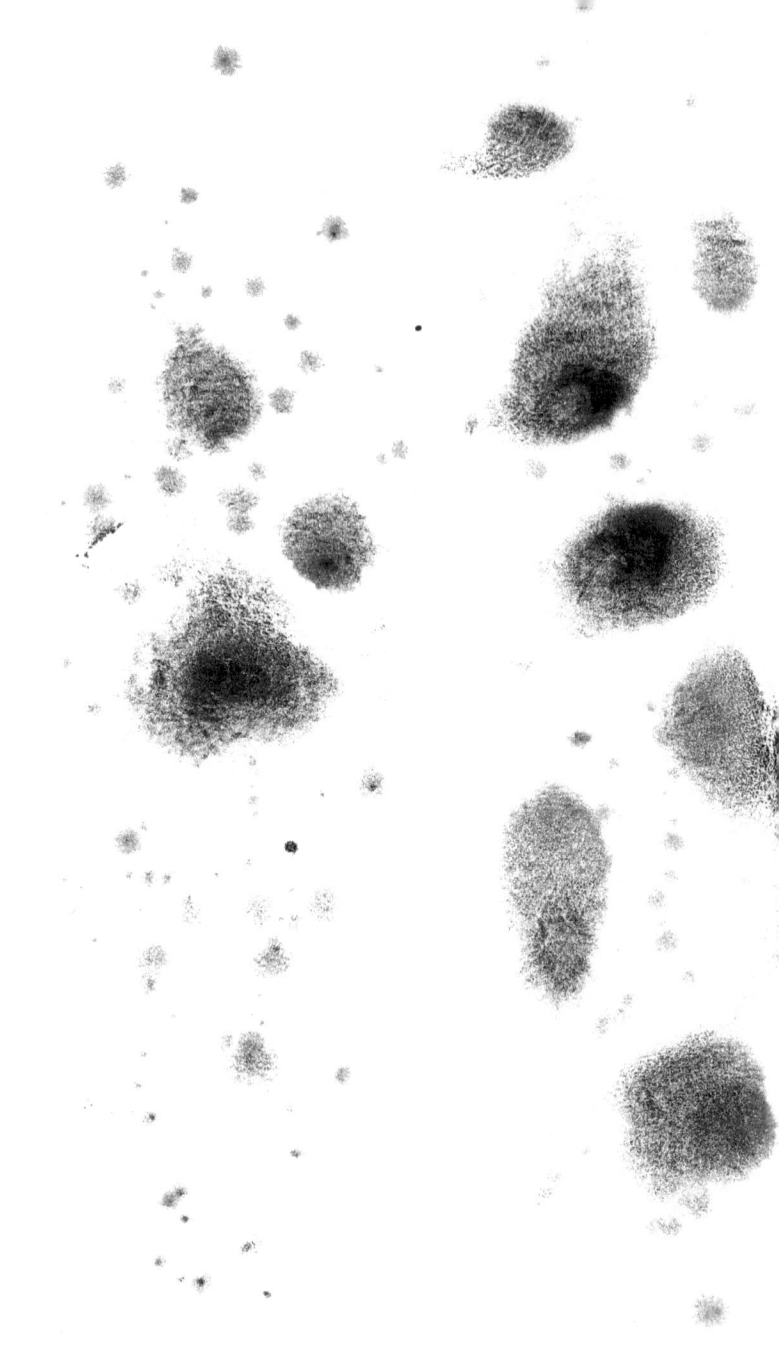

originating

A giant is born pure love.
With a place in this world by right of birth.
A wholeness that is not questioned.
A beauty so deep,
it illuminates all it encounters.

You.

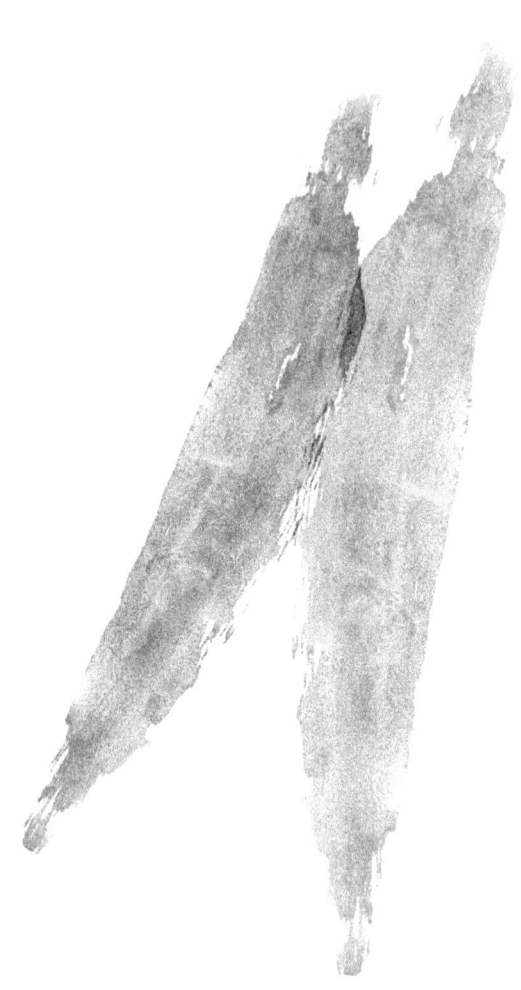

love

Love is a glorious and bewildering mystery. It seems to evade us in times of need only to burst through our barriers in wondrous moments of unexpected heartfelt intensity. Neither occasion makes sense, but it takes us over completely, rendering us bound to its spell.

In times of deep grief, it feels love is the one hurting us.
This very anguish and sorrow may seem as if love is the root of the pain, but in truth it is the conditions of the experience, not love itself, that hurts. It is the grief that aches.

In the confusion around the pain, we build our armour, we dull love's presence, we separate ourselves from the source in order to stay safer. But with a steady practice of belief and acceptance that love is pure, and that love is constant, regardless of our attitudes toward it, the armour dissipates.

It doesn't require anything from us.

Love urgently.
Love unashamedly.
Allow yourself to expand into love, just as love itself, with no hierarchy or limits, expands into you.

Love doesn't need to be performed or perfected, reshaped or researched. Like the air in your lungs, it is available effortlessly, continually, always.

Love just is.

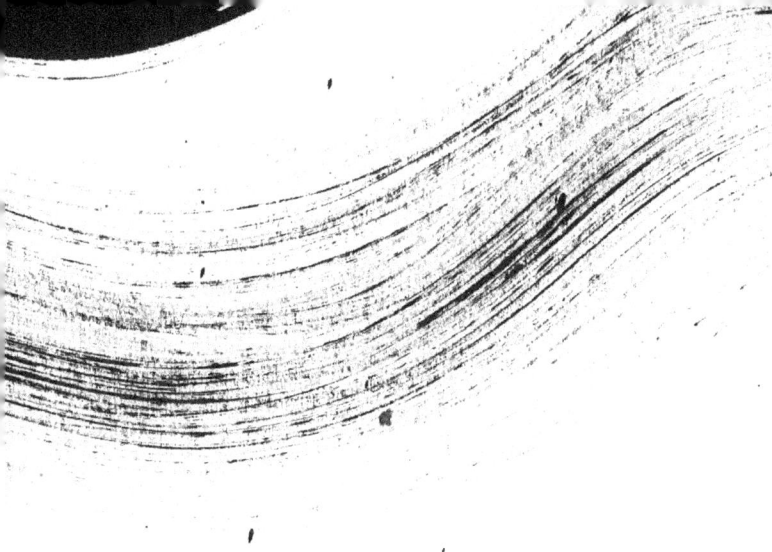

*"For love is the color this place imparts.
Admission is easy, just say you believe
and come to this place in your heart."*

Artist Formerly Known as Prince
Singer

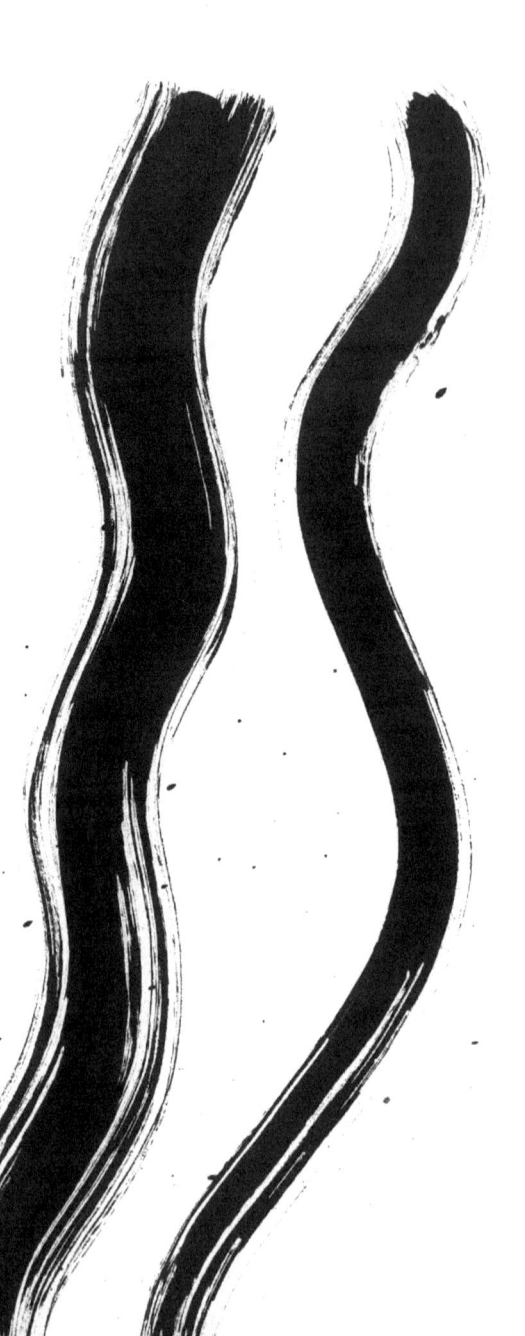

Beauty is invariably confused with vanity. A masked idolised version of ourselves, our bodies, our fashion, all those images that consume us. This pressure to conform to a societal standard is derived from consumerism, and has been enlarged by media, and has taken us away from true beauty.

Real beauty arrives within us as a lens through which we experience a higher expression of life. It helps us see a thing with no judgement: no matter its form, it is precisely how it's supposed to be. No alteration required.

Change happens, and always.
Flowers perish.
Newly painted walls eventually crack.
Smooth skin develops wrinkles.
Rotting smells remind us of the natural process of decomposing.

We wouldn't admonish a tree for changing or evolving. We see each of its seasons as natural and useful. Everything is beautiful within this frame: we are exactly as we are supposed to be.

Everything has its place in the cycles of life.

creativity

Oh, creativity.

You mean the world to me. All that you encompass, I delight in, I revel in.
Because of you I sing out loud, I feel illuminated, my quivering voice speaks volumes.

You bring out the best in me.

You are contagious. When I'm with you, it feels like nothing is, or could ever be, missing.

The thing I love most is that you are so incredibly humble. You never boast.

And you are so capable! It's endearing.

I am so overwhelmingly grateful for you.

I hope you realise how very important you are to the colour of my life, and the progress of our world.

I love you.

Yours,
Giant Me

imagination

Imagination has all the qualities of royalty. It is the most exquisite jewel among the myriad of others. Imagination is pure eminence and the very essence of dreaming.

It lives in those moments of fanciful nature, when a *something* is born from a *nothing*. How delightful!

To make-believe is to dream. Cultivating a dreaming space within allows the powerful freedom to create and spark.
It is a beginning. A possibility.

Being imaginative is special and available at all times. By removing constraint and suspending the word *but* from our minds, much can be brought into life.

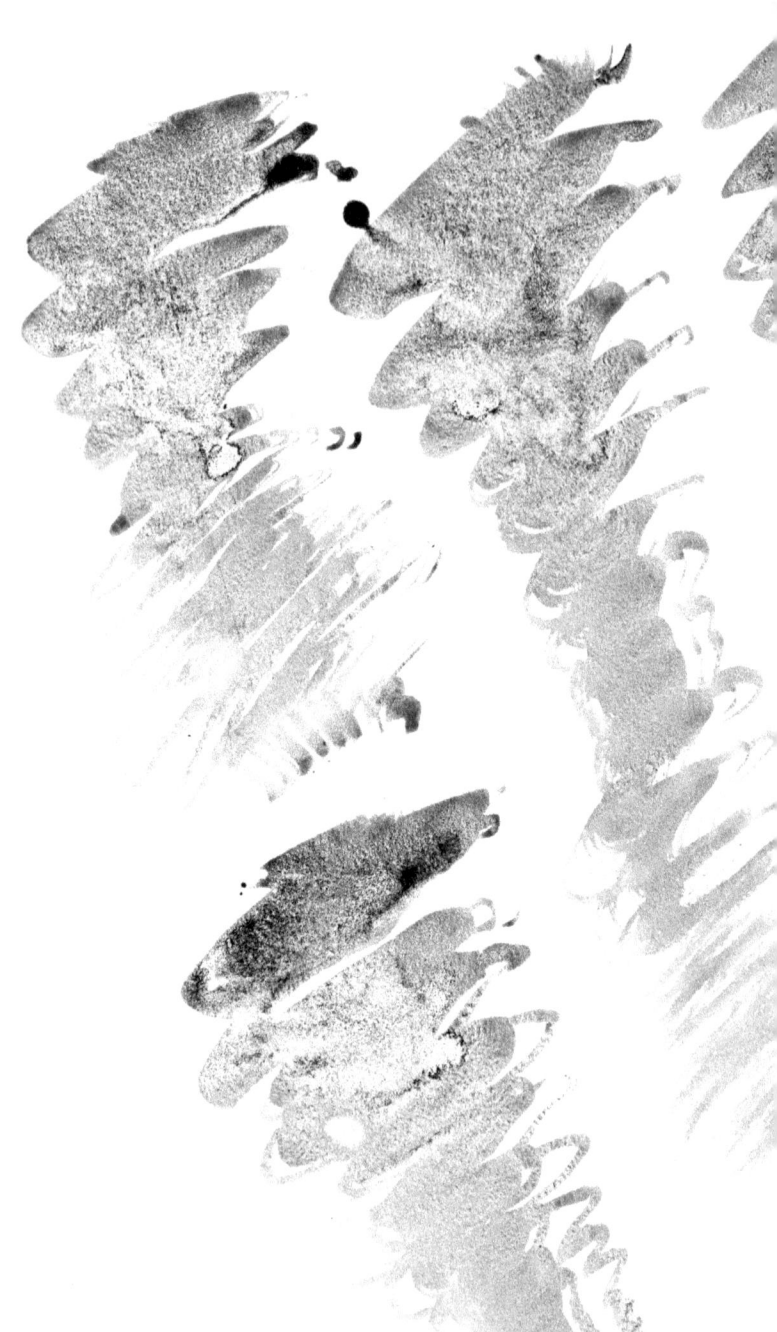

*"I don't know
just where I'm going,
because I've never been."*

Kevin Morby
Singer

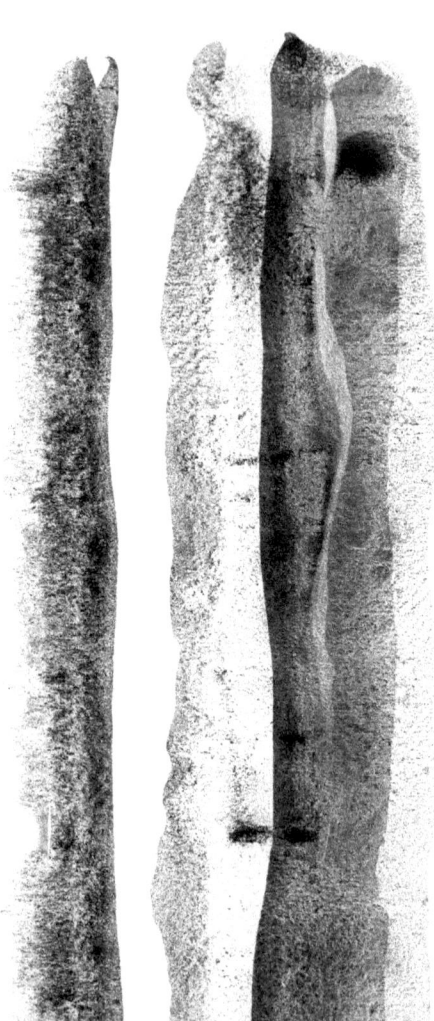

fortitude

Fortitude is like resting into a solid sturdy seat, where we ground ourselves in that which is reliable and dependable within us. It is as unmoving and trustworthy as earthy stone, the carving of which is the shape of our own resilience.

In the seat of fortitude we can endure, and we can withhold. It is a grounded place built from a deep sense of truth, and a respect for one's self, and all that surrounds.

Though strong, fortitude is not stubborn. This heavy stone is simply steadfast. Yielding not to power, but rightness, and in response to the knowing within ourselves.

Fortitude is that wonderful place that holds gentle determination, deep knowing, and the staying power of true courage.

resourcefulness

Resourcefulness is a life force.

Most often resourcefulness is considered an external capability, while its more powerful role is overlooked, that of internal ingenuity. A place that exists *within* to find what is needed.

When there is nothing left, when all resources have been consumed, resourcefulness remains. Its greatest enemy is not in the lacking - the great enemy of resourcefulness is complacency.

Complacency dulls the senses and numbs what is available for solving problems in both the emotional and practical realms.

When all is stripped back, when life feels impossible, exercise imagination, and practise resourcefulness of thought, concept and inventiveness.

Therein lies greatness, hope, and every possibility.

.

Pure joy bubbles up from the simplest experiences in life, but is most often thwarted by our own thinking: our too-high expectations, our too-tight hold on control, our rigid set of conditions we have set for life.

Joy is unveiled when we drop our shields and expectations. The wonderful thing about joy is that when it is felt, it is felt fully. Excitement, awe, promise and beauty are revealed.

Being lost in a joyful moment means letting go, and surrendering to the abundant feelings of possibility, gratitude and wonder.

A moment of bliss that is purely present.

*"Go on fill your heart up
with gladness,
it's not a moment too soon."*

Nick Mulvey
Singer

virtuousness

Virtuousness signifies our worth.

How we live our lives, our moral standards, our choices and our ethics, all reflect who we are.

All too commonly, many have subjugated their own ethics and morals of life, to a governing societal power which doesn't always serve a greater good. Our personal virtue is threatened daily by unwritten rules and expectations, which in turn are fuelled by materialism, consumerism and greed.

To know one's own manifesto in which to live, is powerful. Naturally, unless living separately in a cave is your desire, we all need to work within consensual social, political and economic systems. However, it would be naïve of us to ignore the imposing influence these systems have on us.

Choice of our own standards of living, our beliefs about how to operate in moral integrity may be harder and more complicated than a lackadaisical attitude of life, yet worthwhile if you look to find peace inside your heart, and a healthy community in which to exist.

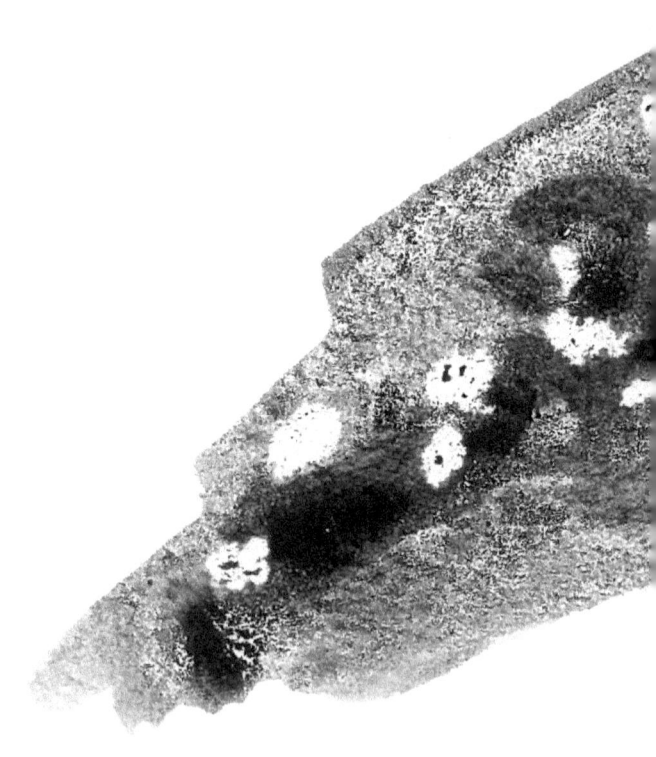

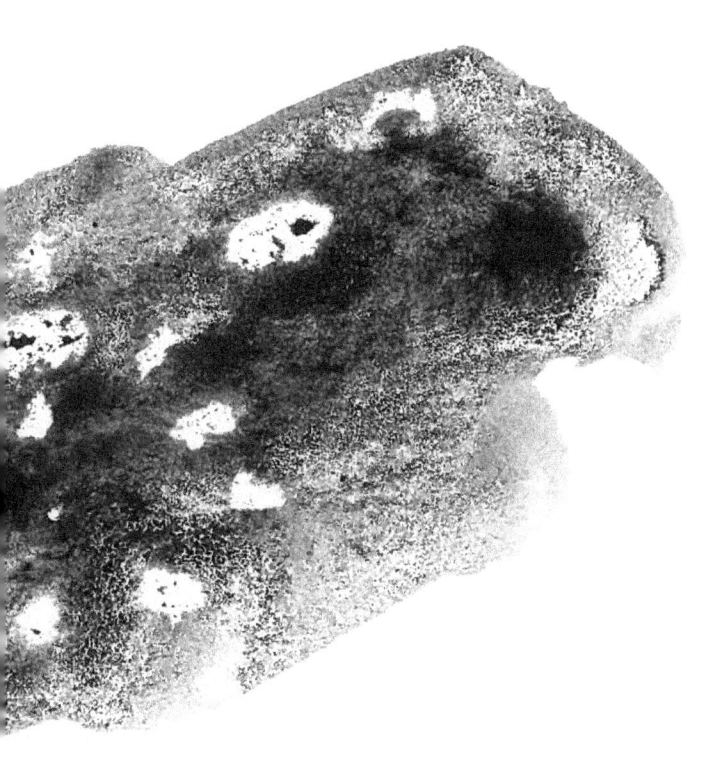

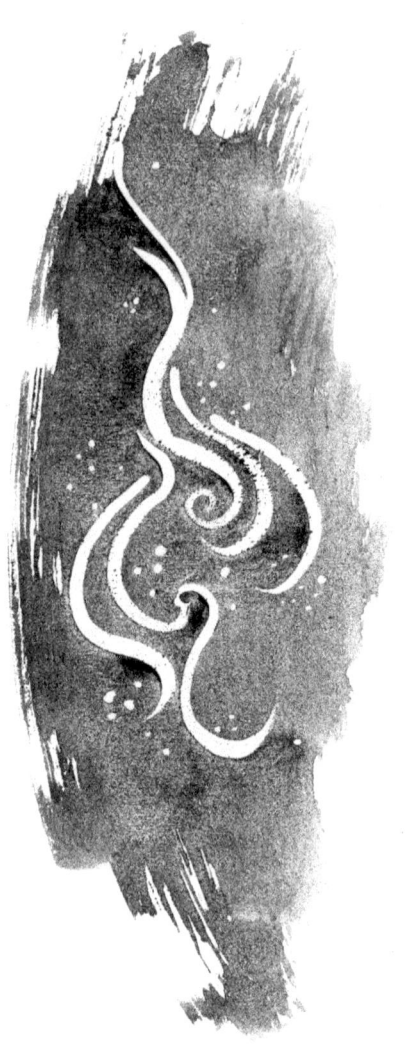

forgetting

We are many giants.

The tiny giant loves to play hide and seek.
The big giant suffers by dulling its internal power.

The sleeping giant dreams into the edges of the soul.
Wondering if it'll ever wake to find the way home.

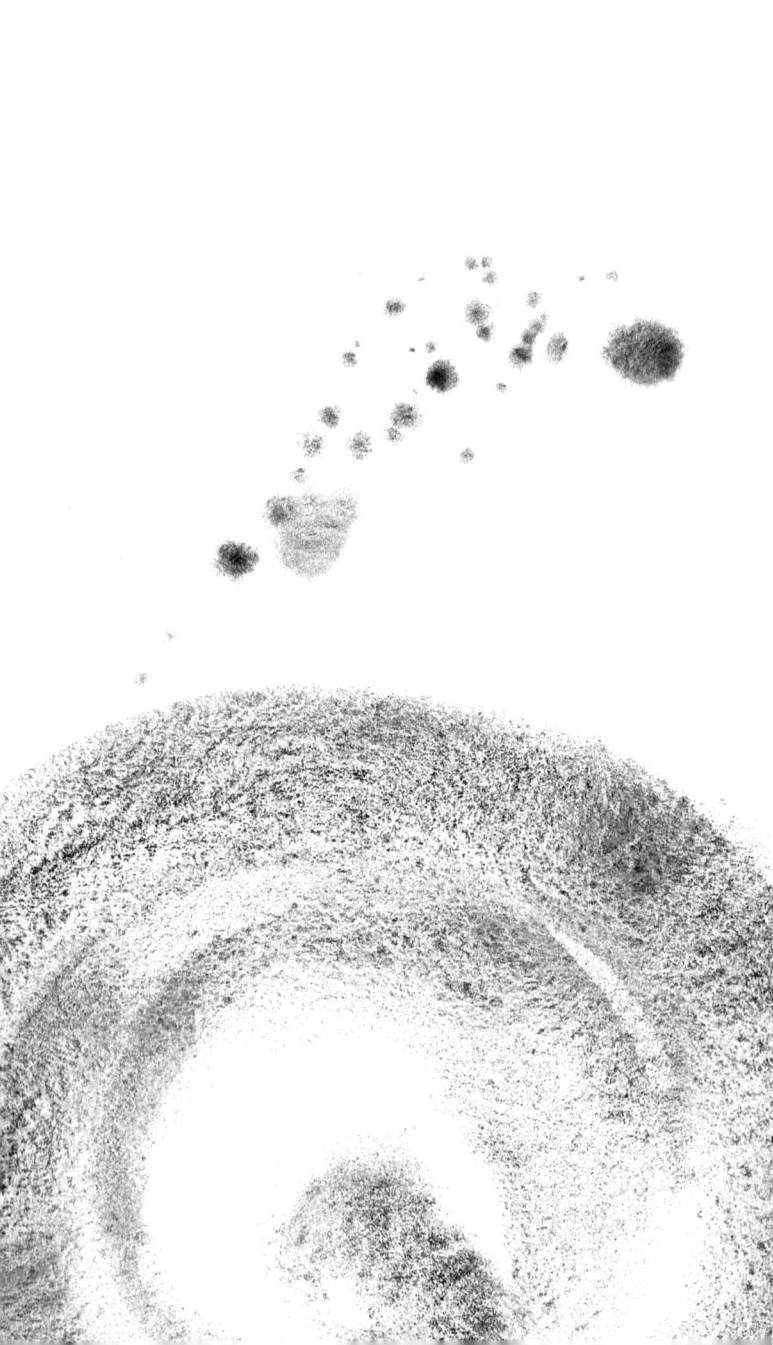

worth

In the absence of worth there is a dark haunting, a recollection of times past when we were told we were not enough, inadequate, deficient, lacking. There are feelings of being cast aside. Lost in a sea of souls, all competing for attention and love.

Sometimes it feels like we must fight for our worth. To have it seen, or to see it for ourselves. To dig it up like a fossil from some distant time, a memory from before, when we had not the worldly cares we have today.

Disappointments, rejections and expectations reign supreme, clouding our judgement of our own worth. Although it's natural for us to look outside of ourselves to gain perspective, we often unintentionally fall victim to comparison, drawing overtly negative conclusions about ourselves.

Worth is innate.

We are born with abundant worth due to the very fact that we were conceived. The mathematical equation for us even having the chance of being born is staggering.

Searching for worth is really a futile endeavour, because it is already present. Always. The challenge is not to discover, but to remember.

It is an uncovering. An unveiling.

Regardless of society, media, parents, lovers, friends or children, you are exactly as you are meant to be. In every changing moment of life, you are worthy of being uncovered. Your uniqueness is a contribution and gift to the world.

You are already magnificent.

betrayal

Betrayal is deceptive due to its crafty illusion that it solely arrives from an external source, a person, place or experience.
Betrayal is deceptive, but not in the way most of us expect.

The common misconception is that all sources of betrayal are *external*. That is, betrayal visits us in the form of another person, a different place, or an experience that was simply *not our fault*.

In fairness, betrayal often does arrive from external sources, but not always, and we need to be aware that there is also a place inside of us that commits this treachery.

We betray ourselves.

We all have internal boundaries, and when we allow those lines to be crossed, it is an act of self-betrayal, a personal treason.

The problem is, we don't even notice our lines are being crossed. In our searching for someone to blame, somewhere else to allocate responsibility, which circumstances were at fault, we set our gaze ever-outward, and we overlook ourselves in the process.

Upon honest self-inspection, we may find that some of our own hard lines, the ones we have drawn for ourselves that represent choice and responsibility, might be missing their foundations. With no patrolling or enforcing, these lines may have become so unclear they can barely be found anymore.

Worth is the voice to heed when self-betrayal is in full force. Specifically, self-worth, that ever-present reminder of our singular value on this earth. In slowness and gentleness, it calls to us to explore ourselves, to draw the hard lines once more.

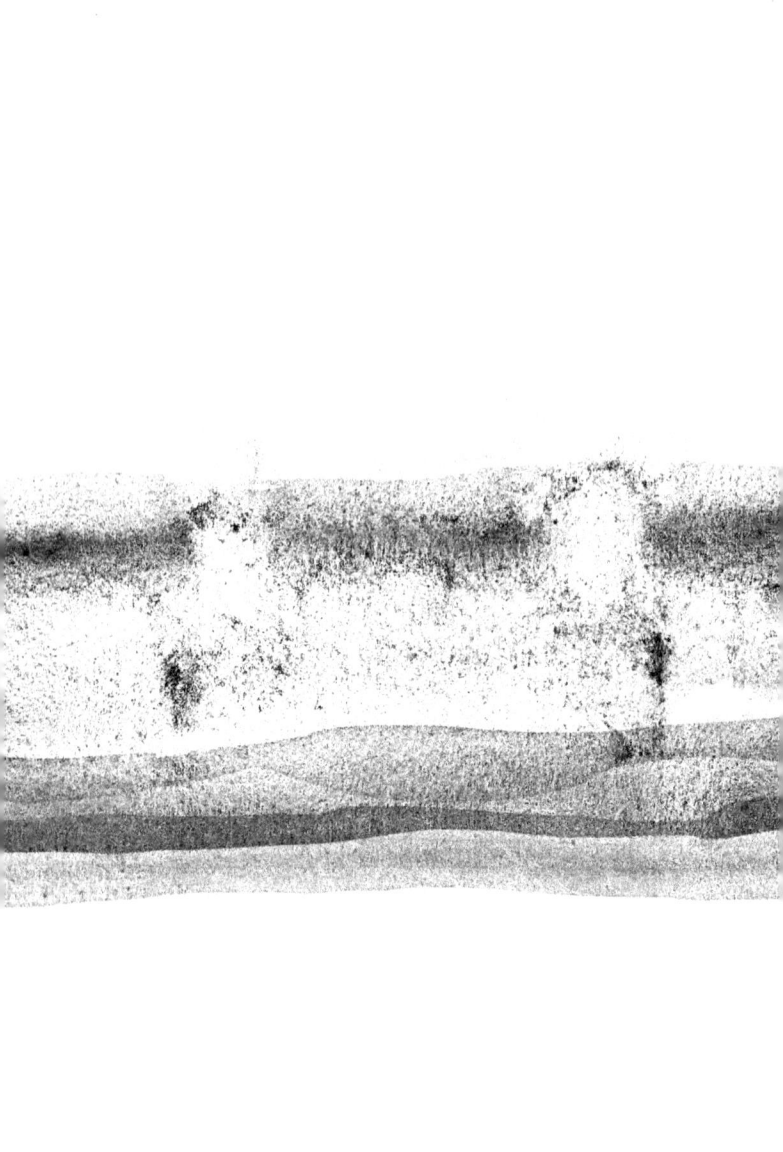

attachment

The moment we were born, we were disconnected.

Everything we knew whilst in gestation - the warmth of the womb, the comfort and certainty of our surroundings – all vanished with the cutting of a cord.

As a tiny person we are destined to rely on another. For safekeeping. For survival. For everything.

As we grow, we become independent – and we rush to do so – seeking our unique identity and distinctive self. In the process, we inherently search for a homecoming: a return to the safety of the mother figure.

Though our minds aren't always aware of our motives, we move through adult life seeking what we once had, in places outside of ourselves.

This longing can manifest itself in unhealthy attachments, obsessions or infatuations. The sense of clinging to an idea, an identity, an object or a person can often indicate the truth: that we long to return to a place and time as whole and pure as when we were born.

Every time we misguide ourselves toward a saviour figure, we relinquish our power. We buy in to the illusion that safety rests *out there* somewhere, separate from and external to ourselves.

Wondrously, the opportunity is always available for us to return to the wholeness, love and peace we feel we have lost. In the natural process of returning to self, we allow our power to return also.
In the awareness and acceptance of our disconnect, we discover how deeply connected we really are.

grief

Grief mimics quicksand dragging us under slowly suffocating and swallowing us whole. We question as we sink into the all-encompassing darkness, is this the end? We fret and flail for we assume once we are in, surely, there is no way out. And at times that very anticipation gives sweet relief.

Grief is suffering. It is an attack on our identity. Who am I, without my career? My health? My loved ones? Amongst these issues, we cannot help but face our own ultimate expiration.

Grief is loss. Along the paths of our lives we also lose our youth, our confidence, our independence, our beliefs, our security. With the goal of our own betterment, we will even deliberately choose to experience loss in order to change.

Grief is forgetting. Over time our truest natures become buried, we forget who we are, and we start to lose pieces of our originating selves.

Grief shapes us. As we acknowledge the pain, the loss and the fear, we are gently released from suffering and beckoned to move onward, fresh breath in our lungs. We realise we are capable even at our lowest ebb, within our deepest sorrow. We learn that we are sufficient even in suffering.

Grief is natural. It hurts, but who said being alive and awake should never hurt? We love, we live and we lose. Grief grants us the opportunity to play all the octaves of the heart.

Imagine a pianist who plays only half of the keys on her magnificent instrument. The music, oh, so less sweet. Playing every emotional note throughout life is a wonderful gift.
So play, my friend. Revel in the rich tones of a full life-song, and know that each note is yours, and each has its own beauty.

*"Fight, like every breath in you's a strike.
From some great fighter in the sky."*

Gang of Youths
Band

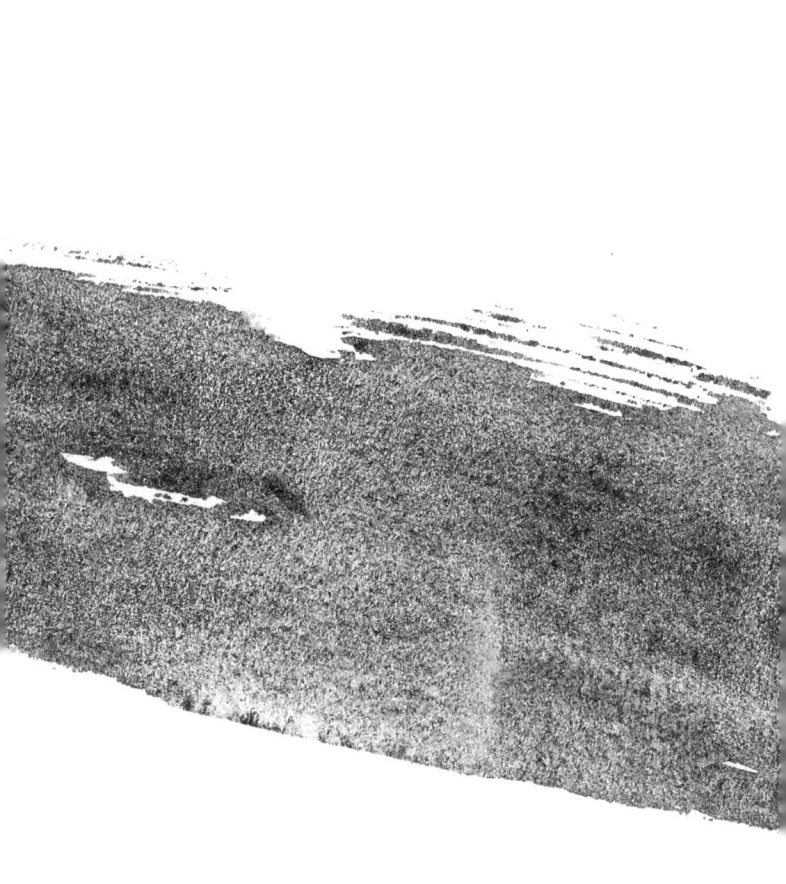

regret

Regret is simply this: you know now what you didn't know before.

If you knew differently you would have done things differently.
You would have acted differently. You would have *been* different.

What we know, and what we have access to at any given time,
is a gift. Even the looking back, the thinking that we
"should have...", is an indicator of our great capacity to grow.

We have learned since then.
We are already changed.

Do not beat yourself up.
Do not waste your days in the mire of regret.
Everything is a lesson and a gift.
Use it all, as wisely as this given time permits.

You are exactly as you are supposed to be in this moment.
As you are in every moment of your life.

blame

We often reach for blame to protect our ego. In those times when life gets too much, when we feel such overwhelming indignation that we just want to scream into the world that life is cruel, and nature itself is against us, blame is a useful device to employ for our defence.

Blame is a good short-term experience of righteousness and relief. It will momentarily focus outward; it will help you understand your boundaries. Your hard line where you have just had enough and blaming someone, or something temporarily, lets you off the hook.

To suggest not to reach for that device, not to blame, sounds harsh. And difficult. The reality is, there are times where others cross our boundaries without our permission, and those experiences are terrible for us. But, blame cannot negate the experiences.
Blame doesn't heal. It simply relinquishes us of our power, and restricts our control of our own healing.

Don't give away power. Stand up for yourself. Stand up for your rights, and for the rights of others. Stand with purpose, draw strength from the sovereignty into which you were born.

Be strong, my friend.
Feel the feelings of anger - you are never denied those rights.
But do not let blame or anger rule you.

Hold fast to purpose, reach deep for moral integrity, and the sheer strength of responsibility will rise, and inevitably favour you,
and you shall prevail.

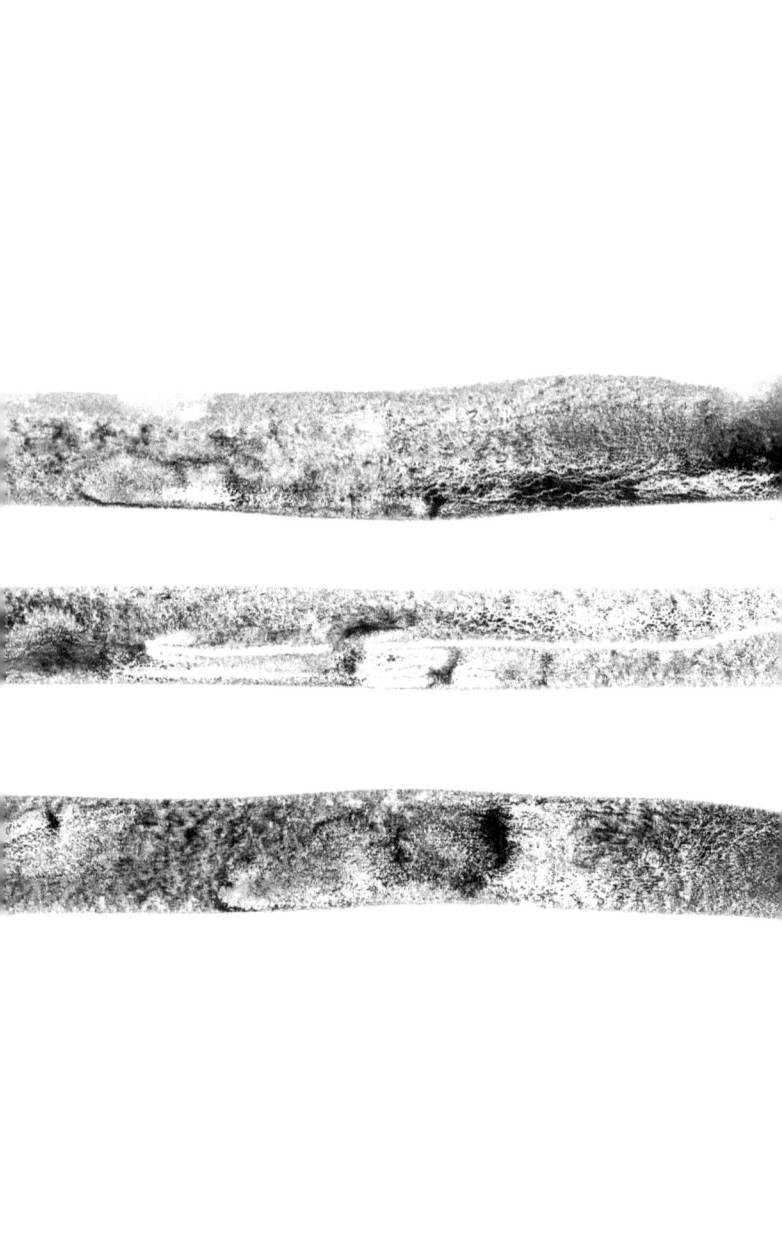

uncertainty

Uncertainty is our ally. It may feel at times like uncertainty leaves us deserted or uncared for. As if the very ground beneath our feet is unstable and won't ever be again.

The beauty in uncertainty is reality. The image of perfection suspended, and this inhibited view provides alternatives and new information. When uncertainty is present, the rigidness of expectation lifts and instead shines a light on newness if we are willing to see.

As our ever-changing nature is at the very cellular level, when we surrender to uncertainty without reeling in the floundering superficial lack of control, letting go brings sweet peace.

Finding a way to negotiate a lack of certainty is to let go of the control, of the fear and doubt, and simply experience the sweet peace that comes with surrender to the unknown. This surrendering is a lifelong practice, the reward of which is a deep, loving certainty, seated firmly in the realm of not knowing.

When you feel perturbed by uncertainty, take a mental step back and acknowledge your expectations, your perceived needs, and then notice your truth about what is present, what is certain, and what was, indeed, always there.

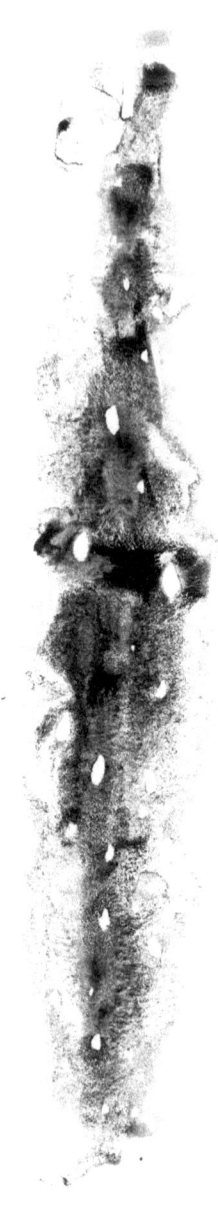

Doubt is the imposter under our own skin.

Triggered by feelings of not belonging, it questions our self-worth, cripples our confidence, and betrays our faith. We forget who we are, and what we are capable of, and are left paralysed and insecure.

In the fleeting moments of doubt, we can generally recover and just keep going. But it's the lengthier periods, where circumstances and lost confidences collide, that leave us rocked and shaken.

Driving away doubt takes courage, and belief.

It is our calling to find *bigger* – to fly higher and see all of life.
To zoom out of the momentary place we find ourselves and envision the entirety of life, the long timeline that exists
behind and beyond us.

As we gaze down upon ourselves, and witness the beautiful lineage of our life, we begin to gain perspective, we can inch ourselves forward another step.

We are not stuck. Though we move slowly, we are moving
none-the-less.

We are more than doubt.
We have been before and will be again.
There is more than this moment.
More than this emotion.
More of you still to explore.

"I will squeeze the life out of you
You will make me laugh
and make me cry
And we will never forget it
You will make me
call your name"

Hunters and Collectors
Band

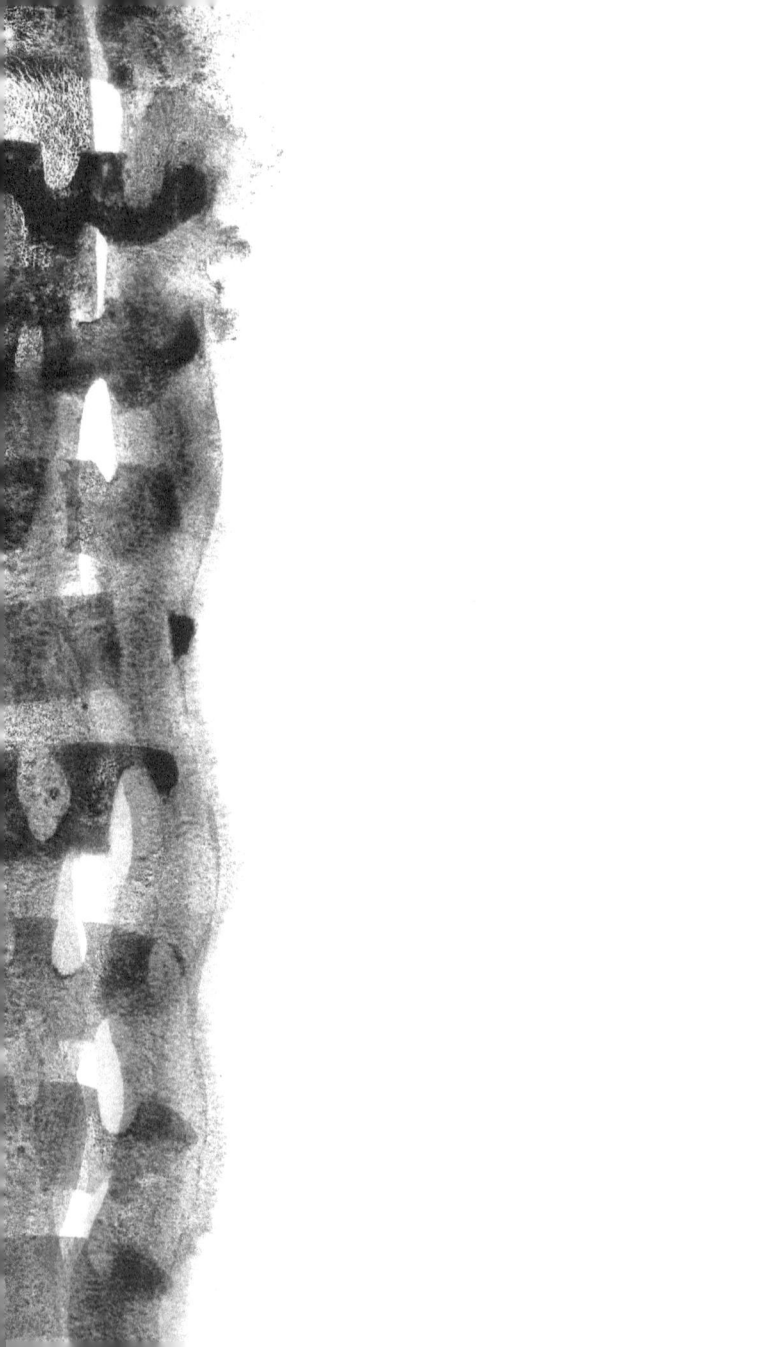

jealousy

Jealousy is a curse that first compels us, then spins us out of control. It is a dark magic that reveals the most brutal, distasteful aspects of our shadow side, like nothing else on Earth. The bitter taste of jealousy, even when fleeting, leaves us desperate, and wanting. It exposes our incompleteness, and uncovers our lack of self-worth.

Jealousy is the hallmark of deficiency. It is derived from a belief that we deserve something, or someone. That we do, or should, possess another. It is an inherent feeling of entitlement, a sense, perhaps, of indignant righteousness.

There are subtle distinctions between Jealousy and her sister Envy. While Jealousy has us believe that something we have should not be taken away from us, Envy convinces us to want something that someone else has.

When we access feelings of jealousy or envy, we disregard our abundant nature. We forget that there is, indeed, enough for everyone. Employing generosity and gratitude can be helpful in countering these tricky emotions.

Over time, and with practice, we can begin to let go of expectation, release our sense of ownership, and exercise acceptance, knowing that nothing is ever ours anyway. We are always transitioning, in a constant cosmic flow.

Know that you are enough. You are a gift.
And not only you, but we, and they.

Appreciating the value of all, greatly aids the cementing our own worth, and our place in life. When feeling a lack, practice the mantra,

"I am enough right here, right now."

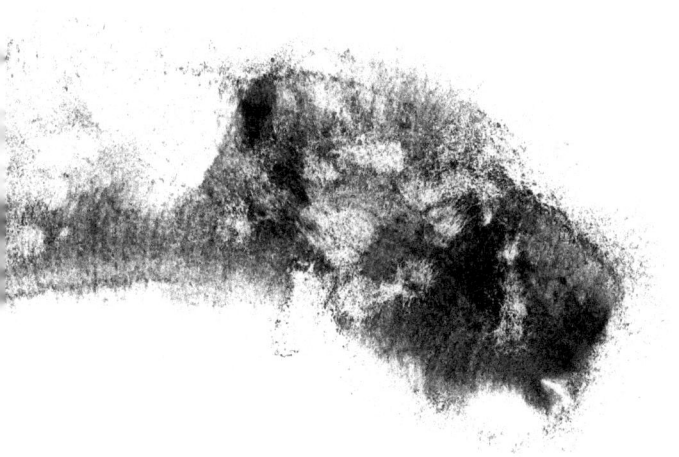

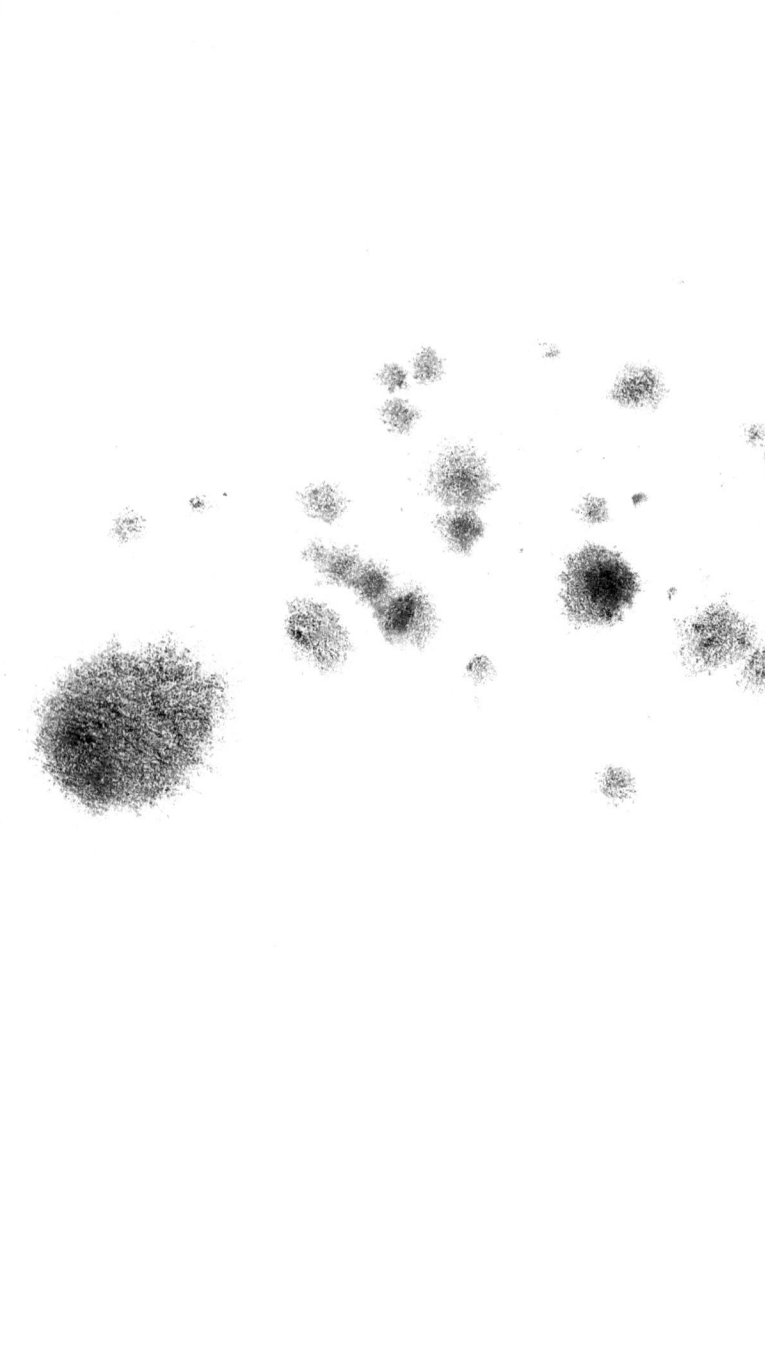

waking

A giant waking may feel cumbersome.
Memories, long stored unfurling.
A deep knowing, permeating from within.
Dormant reasons for sleep no longer binding.
The resonant calling to stir.

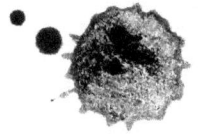

tenderness

Tenderness is an achingly profound empathy. Never rush tender feelings. Never be forceful or punishing or harsh with a soft heart.

Like the cautious prodding and feeling around the edges of a bruise, a cultivated tenderness provides a safe space for self-compassion, where the finest layers of the heart are gently explored.

Tenderness felt fully, opens a portal to truth-telling, and also truth-seeing. A place we ourselves have been hiding from, allowing us to see each other through a softer, more gracious lens.

Tenderness of the heart is an invitation
to feel more deeply, without blame or judgement.

Consider your own hands.
As you pick something up, be gentle, be guiding rather than forcing.
Contemplate each sensation at your fingertips,
and apply these ideals to your heart.

Treat tenderness as you would a child.
For as you already know,
that child is also you.

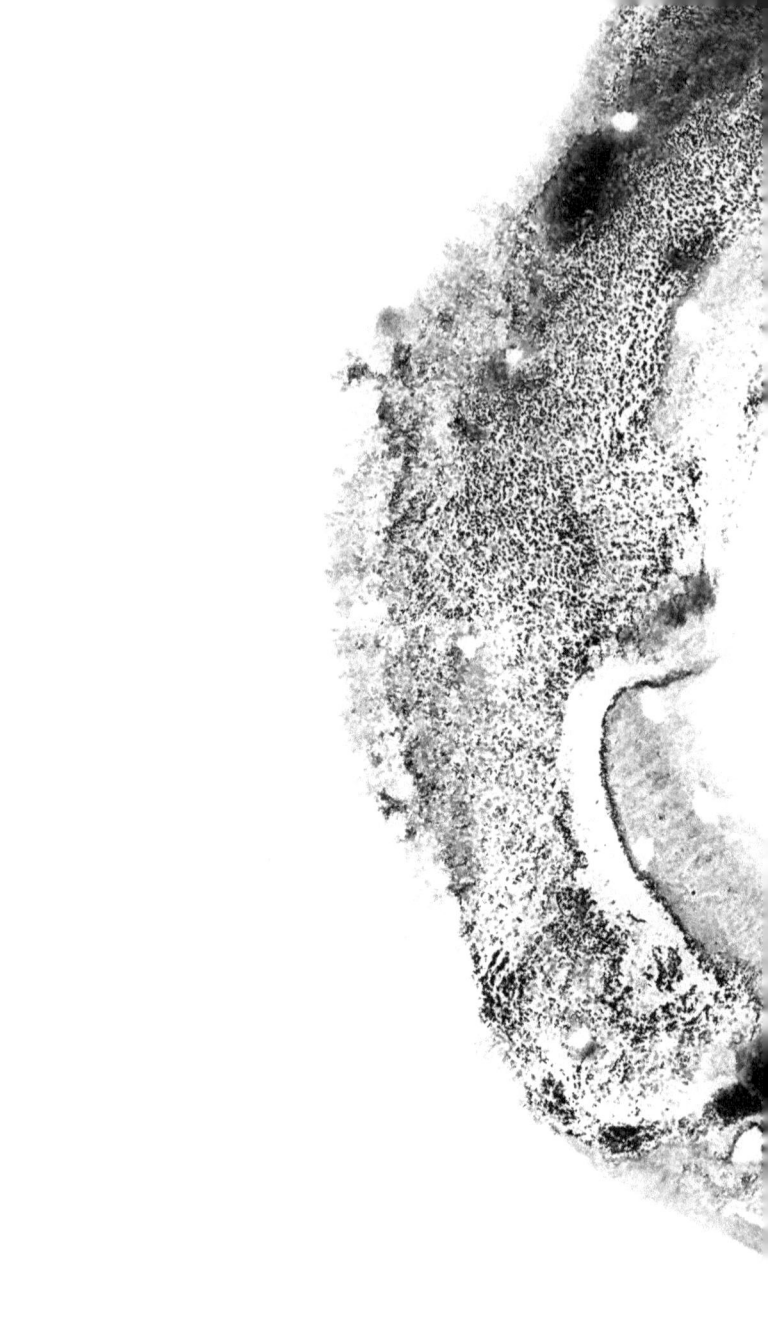

"Lean in beloved friend,
bits of tender reel me in.
Tip the cup and pour the rubies.
Wild laughter, lust, and beauty.
Fine tune me with patience."

Rising Appalachia
Band

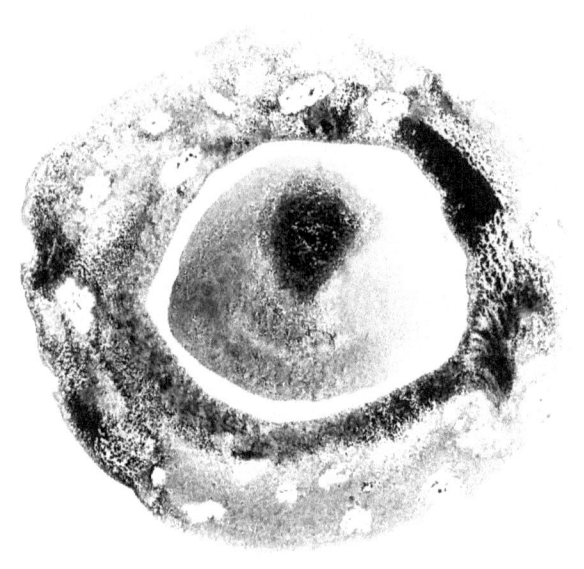

Gratitude is visceral. An expansive sensation of *enough*.

It is a place of pure appreciation and thankfulness, glowing, radiating out of us, shining a light on love itself.

Gratitude is the tonic for times when we have lost control.
It calls us into the present moment of witnessing all that is, as opposed to what may not seem to be. It is a signal that we value the abundance of now rather than what we might catch ourselves expecting.

We become aware of the fullness, and the richness of life.

In its full expression, gratitude brings serenity and ease. It seats us firmly in the timeframe of today, and embraces the universal laws that exist regardless of us.

Gratitude wants for nothing, it simply rejoices in life itself.

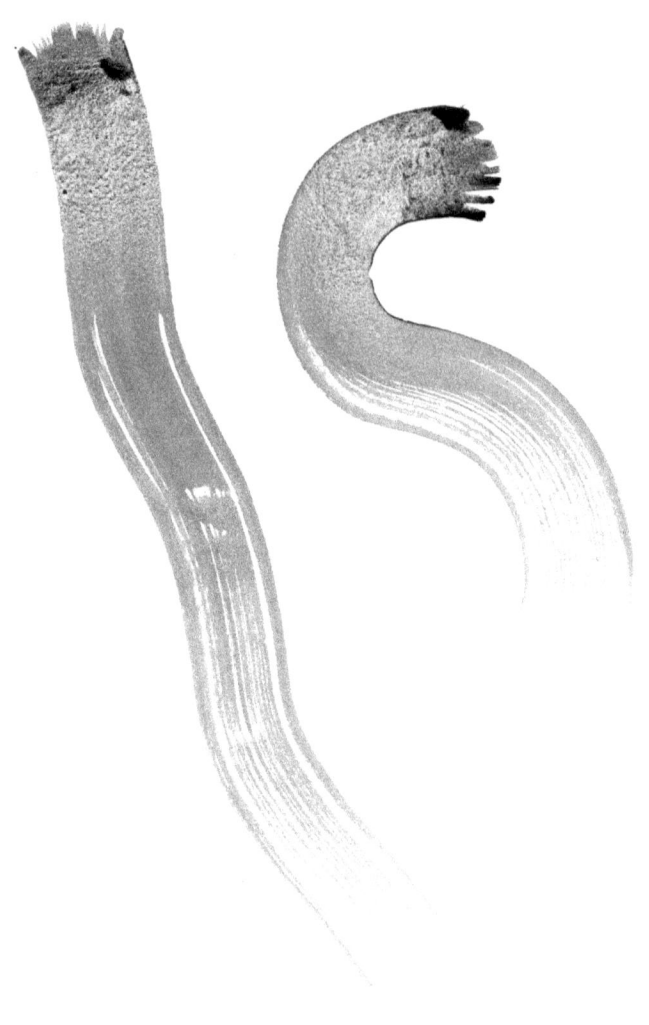

The curious are forever unearthing,
while the non-curious renounce their right to discovery.

When we are curious it highlights our ability to remove the need for unhealthy righteousness. Opening up to curiosity means letting go of perfection, and those stubborn traits that prevent us from changing.

And when we let go, we do not lose our identity, our knowledge or our wisdom. None of those aspects of our self that we rely on for stability are diminished at all. Instead, the space that opens to us, upon our letting go, enables extension, and amplification, of all that we are.

Curiosity breathes new energy into the old.
It works within the spaces of dreams and improvements, of creativity and wonder. It carries an inquisitive essence of learning.

The building blocks of wisdom are born right here, in the gloriously playful and generous practice of curiosity.

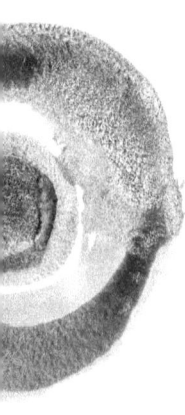

forgiveness

I suspect you know already the true power
of this beautiful and humbling practice.

It's not about them.
Forgiveness is about
you.

What do you think life would be like if we never needed to forgive?

If there was no need of absolution,
because none of us claimed the affront?

If we, ourselves

(you, yourself)

were not offended in the first place?

truth

Facing deep truth is facing the wisdom of your own being. The reality of yourself, and all you encompass.

What is truth, anyway? It lives as close to us as the elements of the natural world, of all the laws of nature. It does not pertain to right and wrong, but something more pertinent. A fundamental knowing that is constant and wholesome.

When we face away from truth, we forgo real. Shields and shadows rise and like a prisoner kept behind bars, limit our potential.

Living in a superficially manufactured illusion, this existential half-life may seem reasonable to the ego, but eventually our own cells will intervene. The very atoms we are made of react to the misalignment of truth. They release all the stresses and untapped feelings, protesting the incongruence.

The harvest of truth is wellness. Comfort comes from knowing the truth. Congruence runs pure, like a deep natural spring, when truth is elevated and abundant.

Deep truth is a sweet remedy for unfulfillment. It allows us a generous consideration of all things, an opportunity to view life unfiltered, uncovered.

Like and *dislike* matter very little here.

The way of truth is the swiftest path to a full life. A life rich with joys and heartbreak, loves and disappointments, pain and healing.

As many before us have ruminated,

"And so it is."

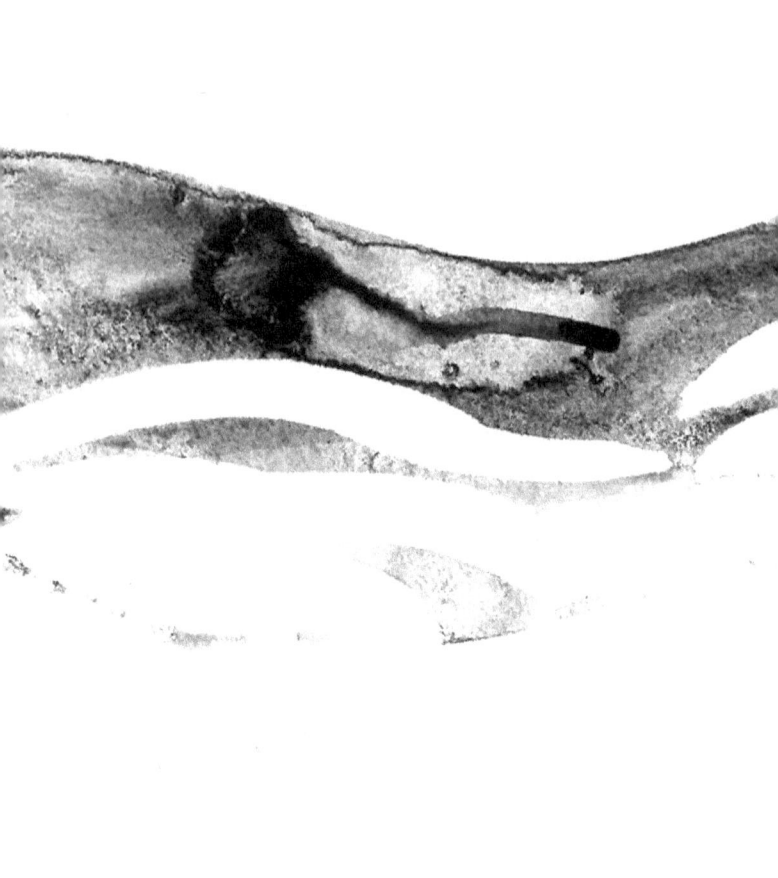

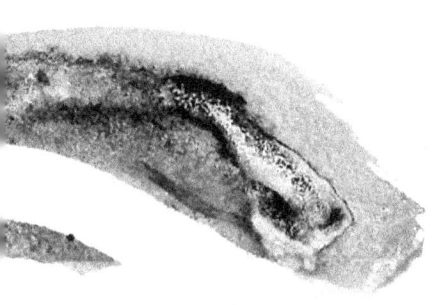

*"We must let go
of the life we have planned,
so as to accept
the one we have waiting for us."*

Joseph Campbell
Writer

Hope exists in two forms.

Intellectual hope is often confused with a fanciful wish and can be painfully misdirected. This type of hope is tainted with *attaining* rather than betterment. It is a logical activity that is fundamentally passive, and frequently destructive.

Profound hope originates in the pure place of yearning.
It is earnest and striving, projecting itself from the depths of our heart to serve both our critical survival needs, and our ethereal dreaming state.

Profound hope trusts that there is always a next day, another chance. It is a faith that life itself is enough. It paves a path well beyond intention, drawing us in to a conviction so strong the very airwaves around us pay attention.

Hope is possibility.
It keeps us alive and it makes us better.

It is a beautiful, deep, eternal longing
for beyond.

wisdom

What is wisdom?
Who would you consider "wise"?

How did you come to those conclusions?
Did they exhibit special qualities or behaviours?
Have you also exhibited some of those qualities yourself?

When next you face a challenge, ask yourself,
"What would a wise person do?"

And then, listen.

aloneness

Loneliness is remarkably dark. A reverberatingly hollow and empty place. Cavernous at times where the solitary experience is simply the echo of one's thoughts.

Loneliness longs for an addition. It is an unsatiated state of being, requiring another person, or object, to soothe and resolve us.

It is also a beautifully natural state. As humans, we desire physical and emotional connection. We are hard wired to be in tribes, to experience union. When we lack such relationships, in our loneliness and isolation we yearn for attention. We long for love, and we seek it from outside ourselves.

A related state of being, also very familiar to us all, is that of *aloneness*. Though strikingly similar, aloneness has a fundamentally different energy.

Ultimately, each of us are alone. The paradox is this: while our *physical* self knows this aloneness to be true, our *spiritual* self understands a deeper truth. That we are, in fact, connected. Across elements, atoms, particles and quanta, across realms and channels not even discovered.

We are always connected. Even when we are alone.

As we cultivate a healthy state of aloneness, we allow our bodies to heal, and our hearts to trust. We return to our selves with less anxious dependence on others.

Waking up to aloneness is an invitation to be still.
To bask in ourselves for a moment.
To deeply witness our own exclusive being.

vulnerability

The magnificent power of vulnerability has always been tarnished by fear, insecurity and the illusion that its existence somehow attests to weakness. We fear appearing weak, so we grip even more firmly to our worldview, and strive to contain our most sensitive thoughts and feelings.

We silence our hearts, telling ourselves that surely, no sane person would purposefully crack open their sacred heart-spaces, and willingly reveal their most private insecurities, flaws and failings.

And yet, that's exactly what vulnerability asks of us. In tiny pieces, or in wide chasms, we lay open our innermost feelings to public observation and judgement.

It takes courage to open up. It's uncomfortable. When we keep ourselves guarded, we presuppose that our fellow humans are not like us. That nobody else has these same awkward, sad, confusing feelings. But the reality is so different.

Our trusted friends can help. They understand, at least as best they can. They too struggle to unveil their inner spaces. No one is immune.

One of the greatest lessons of my life has been this:
To not deprive my trusted people their right to be a true friend,
To hold that space and play their role fully.

We need openness. We need strength and truth.
And we need vulnerability, if only to stem the undercurrent of shame that most of us silently carry.

It is a great privilege to hear another's truth.
Revealing our honest self is never easy, and we will be practicing until the end of time, but know that the practice is worth it, and is needed, and our hearts will be so grateful.

quickening

In a quickening, we find beautiful anticipation.

At our fingertips, the culmination of all that has come to pass, together with the inspired hope of all that will be in the future.

It is stimulus and serenity, combined. A fusing of motivation and intuition, flowing like molten silver, dispensing its alchemic, magnetic qualities into existence.

In the quickening, enthusiasm gains pace and life's cheerfulness skips into action.

The rush of possibility.
Eyes wide, mind alert.
Spirit high.

The time is now.

"But if in your fear
you would seek only love's peace
and love's pleasure,
then it is better for you that you
cover your nakedness
and pass out of love's threshing floor,
into the season-less world
where you shall laugh,
but not all of your laughter,
and weep, but not all of your tears."

Kahlil Gibran
from his book *The Prophet*

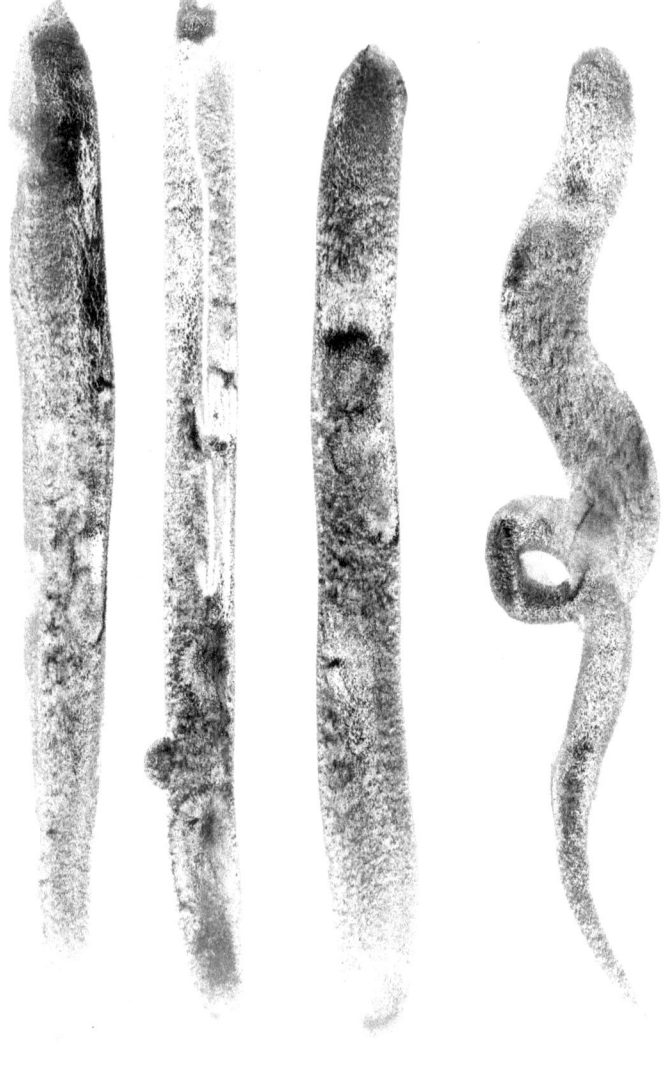

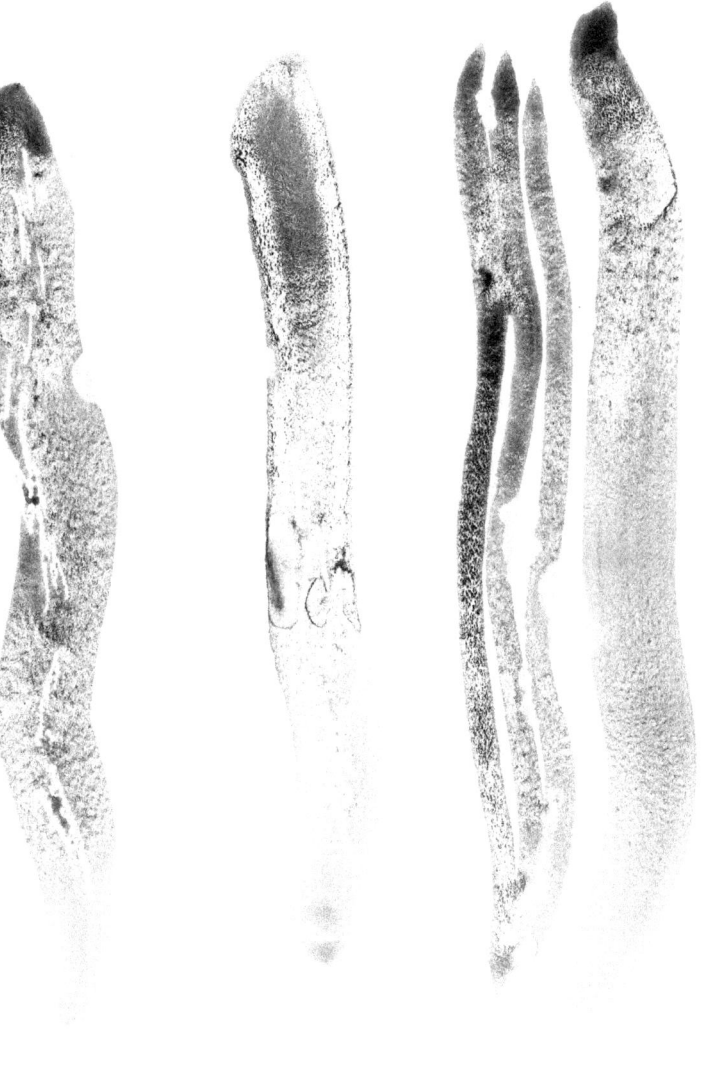

liberating

Oh, those shiny eyes.
That heart so full and light.
Abounding soul.
Risen. Unshackled.
You there!
Your giant has wakened.

empathy

Empathy is perceptive sensitivity. Attuned senses that observe and respect others as they experience themselves. Being grounded in empathy does not mean you lose yourself. It never requires disregarding your own needs.

Empathy honours both you and others in the process.

Echoing a sense of understanding closely relating to your own, helps others feel valued. Empathy grasps concern relating to others and our communities.

Deeply connected compassion often needs no words. Rapport and regard are identified at a molecular level.

Often when we are connecting with others, our logical mind interferes with our compassionate heart, ambushing us with repetitious algorithms of thought and rationalisation.

Trusting in our own intuition is imperative here, as it senses intensely and broadly. It is a gift to those receiving our undivided attention. And even more valuable to our own development throughout life, as we learn.

Empathetic people grow. They absorb and accumulate wisdom through others. They are nurturers, providers and carers.

Empathy's wonderful comfort is knowing that we can live together, that we exist in a cocooned network, and are never disconnected from the wholeness of humanity.

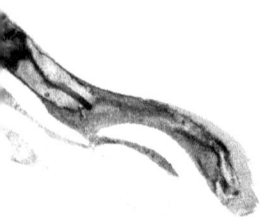
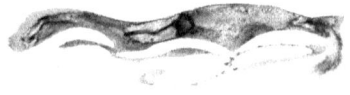

Kindness is profound regard for all things.

Showing both gratitude and compassion.
Reminding us that others suffer.

Kindness seeks no return.
Only to fill another's cup.

Kindness is listening.
Listening with every cell of our body.
It is not distracted.
Or inattentive.

Kindness is integrity.

Considerate.
Careful.
Caring.

Human.

playfulness

Playfulness has a delightfully cheeky energy to it. A youthful feeling which too often we bury under the more mature aspects of our self.

Playing is freedom.
To smile, laugh and explore.

Playfulness is a spring of life, exuding colour, spontaneity and delight. It generates happiness, and then turns contagious.

Playfulness has its own unique wisdom, and dances between the starkest polarities of life. It draws seriousness to the sideline, and introduces jest and fun, infusing light-hearted joy and a much-needed simplicity of being.

generosity

Beyond money or material,
Generosity is flow.

An exchange of spirit.

Greater than I
Grander than You
Giving of heart.

Unlimited
Unbound
Unconditional.

Magnanimous
Benevolent
Charitable.

The ultimate gift.

discernment

Discernment has a noble underpinning, a just and majestic air.

We have all experienced a time where our judgement has been clouded. Where it was hard to discern right from wrong, good from bad, and the consequences were less than desired.

Being discerning in character slows us down and softens our confrontations. We allow the revealing nature of the situation to unfold.

When we act forcefully, we miss things – intricate details containing the next steps on the path. Missing these steps, we forge ahead, but lack the depth or rigour that the diligence of discernment would have awarded us.

Accessing a place of good judgement requires faith in our own intuition. We must trust the subtle nuances, heed the insights, avoid the pressure to rush our way forward, and allow ourselves the patience to arrive at decisions wisely and coherently.

Much is gained by pacing, patience and intuition.

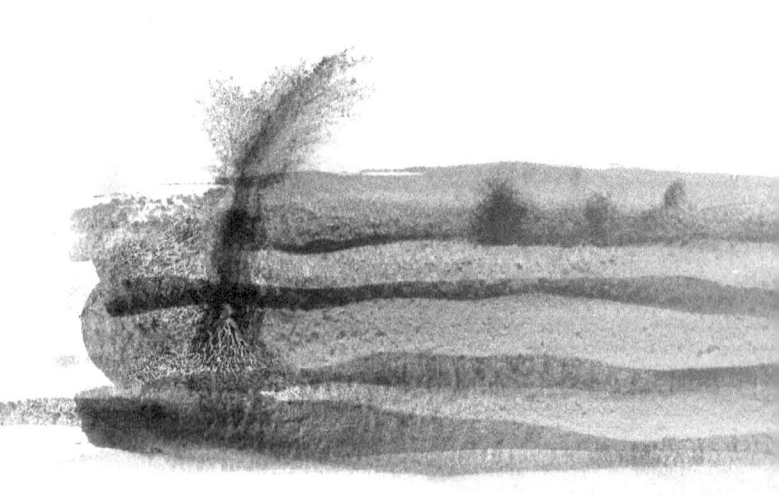

responsibility

You are not an island.

Surrounding you is a deep web of connection that exquisitely intertwines us all. Within the ecosystem of humanity, the animal kingdom and the natural world, is an extensive network. Multiple layers and connection points all around us.

Responsibility first requires an appreciation of these layers, a recognition that everything in our expansive world is integrated. Together, we are a whole.
This recognition, coupled with the reality of how we lead our lives, how we contribute to those around us, and how we relate to our environment, lays the groundwork for true responsibility.

We are cause, and we are effect.

Who we are and what we do carries a multitude of consequence. Taking responsibility for our thoughts and behaviours is an acceptance of this truth.

Responsibility is moral regard for self and others. It requires steadfastness and integrity to act within that sacred realm of knowledge of what is right and true.

Be present and aware.
Know your standards in life.
When you contribute to wholesome actions right now, in this moment, you are also contributing to the greater network, in this moment and the next.

And you set a clear path of intention for all of our futures.

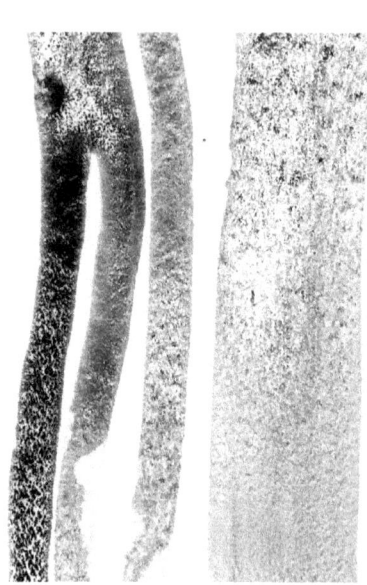

fairness

Injustice hurts.
The sting of not being listened to, acknowledged or validated speaks to the most wounded parts of us. For those who carry a deep historical hurt, a lack of fairness can send us reeling. We feel taken advantage of, used or irrelevant. These feelings may then trigger memories of our upbringing, and magnify those parts of our unloved childhood selves that had long ago drawn the conclusion that "I was just not enough."

All of us, countless times in life, have been judged, blamed and cast aside. In those moments of despair, we hope for a hand to guide us. We seek a steady grip of reinforcement.

And sometimes, that hand appears. It arrives like fortitude and steadfastness, a balanced grounding force that implements the justice we desired, and returns to us the sense of legitimacy we craved.

Fairness is important. It is a fundamental human right, an unspoken pledge of equity in our humanness. It is not about having the same as everyone else, but seeks to ensure each person receives what they need. No bias, no judgement, just pure acceptance that each human warrants what is fair and just.

When fairness is truly in effect, we shine a light on *what* is right, rather than *who*.

A giant awake knows the deep importance of fairness to all.

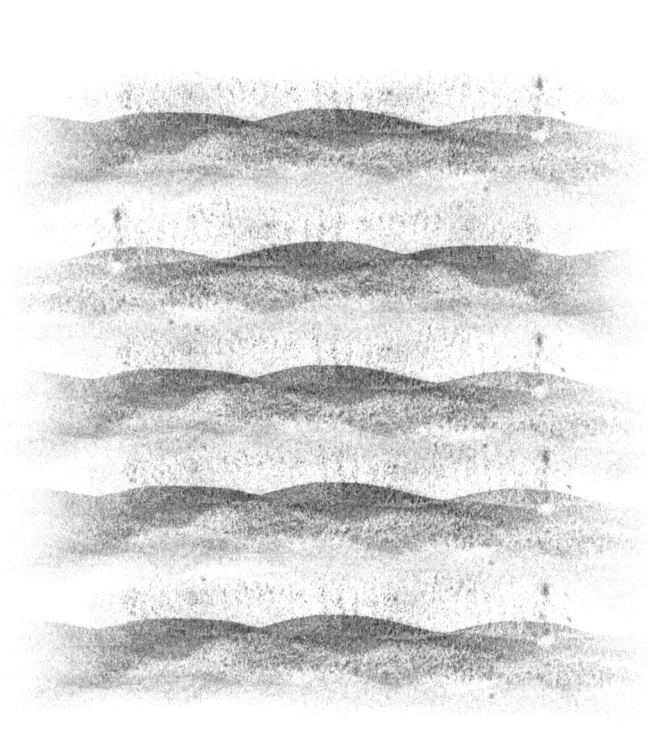

Serving is the great gift of life.

The graceful act of helping evokes a spectacular reciprocity in the eco-system around us.

Every contribution energises humanity, from the tiniest gestures of intent to mammoth acts of service. Heartful, generous acts link us together.

The spirit of serving a fellow human communicates unspoken volumes of respect, value and regard.

When serving from a place of purity, there is nothing required in return. It is a simple and pure gift of time or resources, and it changes the course of another's experience.

Altruism is never left without a form of reciprocity.
When we engage with service, we are engaging with the deepest parts of our soul, within which, we hear the voice of inner fulfilment whisper:

"You are spending the moments of your life with honour."

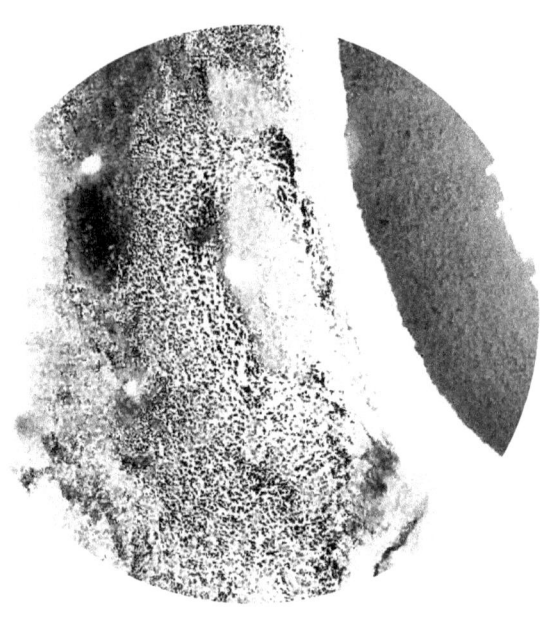

"As the morning gathers a rainbow,
I want you to know now,
that I'm a rainbow with you."

Finley Quaye
Singer

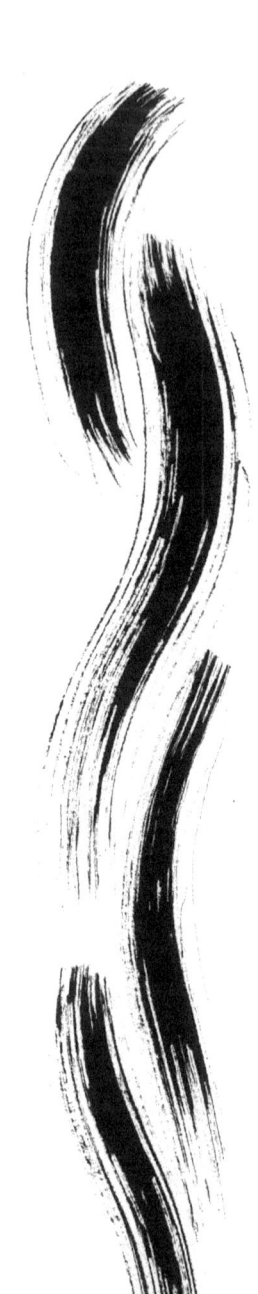

calling

Being called to life indeed takes a hero's journey. As we open ourselves to life's opportunities, we are given the most exquisite invitations to walk the various paths before us. When we hear the call, we may flinch, and turn away. We may try and avoid it, for we know a giant journey like this is never easy. And like a disturbed and fitful night, our lives become a delusion of deep sleep, all the while unsleeping and ill-rested.

Opening up to the reality of the call takes courage, and determination. Walking these unchartered paths requires every facet of life to be experienced. Every possible emotion will be tested. The paths are turbulent and some even treacherous. But they are real.

Life is not meant to be a constant struggle, but it is meant to be full. And with fullness comes all the colours of the rainbow. The beauty and richness within the prism of a rainbow requires both rain and sun to be present. Only then can it reflect itself into the world.

Take chances. Reveal truths.
Dream dreams and dare to act on them.
Try. Fail. Learn.
Use your voice. Expand your heart.
Love anyway.

Look to the horizon and see that the entire universe is ready to respond.

Friend, I speak now to your heart.
Please live all of your life.
Feel everything.
Heed the call.

For when you reach your final sleep,
your giant will have had the adventure of a lifetime.

Say it's here where our pieces fall in place   Any rain softly kisses us on the face   Any wind means we're running   We can sleep and see 'em coming   Where we drift and call it dreaming   We can weep and call it singing   Where we break when our hearts are strong enough   We can bow 'cause our music's warmer than blood   Where we see enough to follow   We can hear when we are hollow   Where we keep the light we're given   We can lose and call it living   Where the sun isn't only sinking fast   Every night knows how long it's supposed to last   Where the time of our lives is all we have   And we get a chance to say   Before we ease away   For all the love you've left behind   You can have mine.

.

Call it Dreaming - Iron & Wine Band

for the reader

I found myself writing in the early hours of most mornings, before the day's thoughts took over and my mind confused me.

Nestled in my bed, I'd watch the sunlight fill the room, turning the walls to honey. For a brief moment I would leave my warm covers and venture out for coffee, only to return to my cocoon, to wake up my very own sleeping giant, and together we would fill these pages.

Throughout the day, I would wander through life, listening to music and having deep conversation. And I would collect moments, memories, storing them ready for the following morning. I wrote about each topic as I felt it. It was almost as if, during sleep, the swirling nature of emotions and dreams inhabited me, and in those early morning moments I'd feel my deepest dark-and-light inspirations.

I genuinely hope that these words help.
It may seem extravagant to tell you this,
but I want these words to be true for you,
as much as for myself.
Each of us is special, and important.

This book changed my life. It helped me be the giant I am, and my wish is the same for you.

Our world is better when we each step fully
into the giant gift of life.

Much love,
Suzanne

for my friends

Thank you, Nathan Maddigan, for falling in love with this book as much as I did. Your cleverness, feedback, empathy, understanding of humanity, and incredible knowledge of storytelling has helped the heart of my writing find its strongest heartbeat. You held a creative container for me to express the best of myself. You are a magnificent human.

My darling Natalia Fidyka. The feel of this book is enhanced and takes a life of its own because of your artful mark. That beautiful conversation we had about art matters, will forever hold a special place in the lineage of my life. You inspire me daily to shine my true light, just as you do yours. There isn't an artist or friend in the world I would have rather paint the pages of this book.

To the humble, selfless, wise soul, Christopher Makokha. I remember so fondly a profound conversation in the heart of Kenya. You told me a story about sleeping giants. That instant I knew the title of this book. You taught me many things, and perhaps the most important notion in life. Deep Hope. Asante sana rafiki.

To Susan Saleeba and everyone at Nakuru Hope and Gabriel Learning Centre in Kenya. My time with you all can only be described as life changing. Your spirit, faith, tenacity and generosity know no bounds. You showed me life. I am by your side. You have my love. Asante sana.

To Fiona, thank you for showing me life, in the face of death.

To my friends, my tribe. Ah, the moment where I lose my words.
I couldn't exist without you. You mean everything to me.
You've taught me everything I know and feel.
I love you.

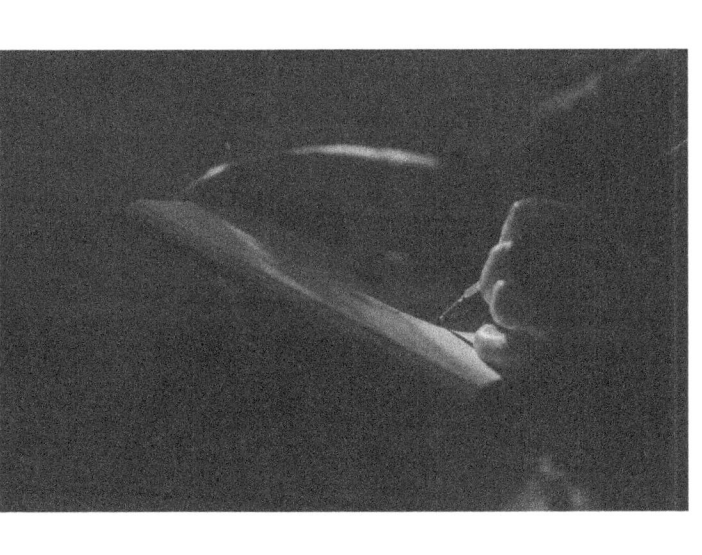

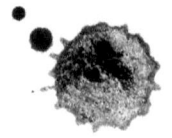

about the artist

Natalia immersed herself in these words, with a beautiful intention to trust what emerged. In conversations between writer and artist, the paintbrush made its simple marks, and in turn made this book extraordinary.

Australian born to polish parents, Natalia Fidyka is a psychologist, gestalt psychotherapist and artist, living by the Indian Ocean in Fremantle, Western Australia.

Natalia delights in facilitating transformational creative workshops, connecting women to nature, to the sacred, and to their own magnificent true selves.

Her core belief is that loving kindness for self and others is the key to healing, and she lives in deep gratitude for family, friends, the cosmos, nature, therapy, creativity and soul food.

As she meanders through the sunlit bushland of home, it seems colour and creativity accentuate her entire life.

Her art studio is a temple, and the creative process is an act of devotion and communion with the very life force of creativity permeating its way through the whole universe.

www.nataliafidyka.com

about the author

Suzanne Waldron was born in England, and lives in Western Australia. She is fascinated with humanity and how we relate to ourselves and one another.

Born deaf, she had multiple operations to restore her hearing. She lived in a truck travelling Europe before becoming a foster child, then homeless teenager. She experienced a tough upbringing. This led her to dig deeply into life's array of emotions and how we can each utilise all that living has to offer. Her first book *A Flourishing Mind* takes the reader through her life experiences and learnings via harsh realities, to a place of deep hope.

Today, she is a behaviouralist having studied a Master's Degree in Coaching and Neuro-Linguistics. Her research focussed on pro-social leadership and the psychological aspects of inner fulfillment through moving significant ideas (beyond self) into action. She studies philosophy and economics to widen her knowledge on meaning and the systems we live in and finds solace in painting as a creative outlet.

Believing that honest, hopeful and truthful relationships are the bedrock of fulfilment and progress, Suzanne works with individuals, organisations and influencers to build cohesive relationships in community, government and not for profits. She works globally combining her skills as a behavioural change facilitator, artist, writer and speaker.

Suzanne is a curator for TEDxPerth and the Museum of Freedom of Tolerance. She is an active ambassador for
R U OK? and Nakuru Hope.

She was nominated for Western Australian of the Year 2016 for her work in the community.

www.suzannewaldron.com

www.ingramcontent.com/pod-product-compliance
Lightning Source LLC
Chambersburg PA
CBHW062051290426
44109CB00027B/2790